Mind Your Own Damn Business

The Greatest Lessons The Music Industry Taught Me About Business

Kevin Ross

Copyright © 2017 RadioMan Publishing Inc

All rights reserved. No part of this book may be reproduced or transmitted in any form or by any means, electronic or mechanical, including photocopying, recording or by any information storage and retrieval system without written permission of the publisher, except for the inclusion of brief quotations in a review.

Table of Contents

INTRODUCTION 1
   A LITTLE BACKGROUND ABOUT ME 2
   ILLUSTRATION 1: MY BOYHOOD HOME ON THE EAST SIDE OF BUFFALO, NEW YORK. TODAY IT'S USED AS A STORAGE UNIT FOR OTHER APARTMENTS 2
   MOVING TO LA 6
   NO EXPERIENCE IS A BAD EXPERIENCE IF THERE IS AN EDUCATION BEHIND IT 10
   STARTING MY BUSINESS… 11
   NOT PAYING RENT 15
   THE END OF THE BULLSHIT 17
LESSONS IN BUSINESS 21
   DON'T FOLLOW THE LEADER, BE THE LEADER… 21
   DON'T ALLOW PEOPLE TO PIMP YOUR BUSINESS 23
   IT'S ALL IN THE PRESENTATION… 25
   BEWARE OF HIRING FRIENDS 26
   TAKE A VACATION 33
   PEOPLE DON'T (WON'T, CAN'T) SEE WHAT YOU SEE 39
   STOP TAKING PEOPLE WHERE THEY DON'T WANT TO GO 40
   YOU WILL FRUSTRATE YOURSELF 40
   IT'S NOT YOUR JOB TO SAVE THE WORLD 41
   IF PEOPLE ASK FOR YOUR HELP THEN DON'T USE YOUR IDEAS, MOVE ON 42
   LOOK AT WHAT YOU ARE PRODUCING. ARE YOU UP TO DATE? 42
   STOP USING YOUR TENURE 44
   USE SOCIAL MEDIA NETWORKS 46
   STOP COMPARING YOURSELF TO OTHERS 47

UPSELL YOUR CURRENT CLIENTS	48
HOW CAN YOU IMPROVE?	48
SEND OUT AN EMAIL BLAST	49
ATTEND CONFERENCES WHERE YOUR CLIENTS GO	50
GET A FEATURE IN A POPULAR BLOG IN YOUR FIELD	50
GET TESTIMONIALS FROM SATISFIED CUSTOMERS	51
CREATE WIN/WIN/WIN SITUATIONS...	53
STOP HIRING PEOPLE WHO NEED A JOB!	54
DON'T BE AFRAID TO ASK FOR WHAT YOU WANT…	56
WHY IS IT SO HARD TO FIND GOOD PEOPLE?	58
ENJOY THE FRUITS OF YOUR LABOR	59
TAKE CARE OF YOURSELF, HAVE A "ME" DAY	62
GROW YOUR BUSINESS…	63
ELIMINATE PEOPLE WHO DRAIN YOUR MENTAL RESOURCES	65
TALE OF TWO LEGENDARY RESTAURANTS; ONE THAT STILL IS AND ONE THAT WAS.	66
AVOID DOING "FAVORS" IN BUSINESS	74
BARTER ONLY WHEN THE BENEFIT IS GREATER TO YOU	78
REASONS YOU SHOULD NOT DO FAVORS IN BUSINESS	80

Mind Your Own Damn Business
INTRODUCTION

Any entrepreneur will tell you that running a SUCCESSFUL business can be both rewarding and very challenging; you are literally married to your business. You may not have much of a personal life or balance because running a SUCCESSFUL business can become an addition, butas time goes on, you will become more accustomed to what it takes to run a business, which includes being able to delegate and hire the right people, keep your sales intact and continuing to educate yourself in your industry so that you can grow. It's a herculean task, and not everyone can do it, but I have noticed that those who are not fully committed don't reap the rewards, and they continue to struggle. Who will you be? The one that struggles or the one that succeeds? It's up to you. Your business can make, break, build you or even KILL if you if you are not careful. I have seen it happen.

Here are my best tips or avoiding costly mistakes per my being in business for 22 years and having a successful first business venture. The music industry has been an extremely igreat educator for my growth, client relationships and mistakes.

A Little Background about Me

Illustration 1: My boyhood home on the East Side of Buffalo, New York. Today it's used as a storage unit for other apartments

I grew up in the Town Garden Apartments on the east side of Buffalo New York. While not considered "projects" in the 60s thru the 80s it was still the ghetto, but I didn't know it. I didn't know it UNTIL I finally left in 1983. All I knew was that I hated it. I hated most of the people, the thinking, th e

Mind Your Own Damn Business

way I was treated the lack of dreams and goals and the extreme negativity. I thought it was me until I went to Atlanta, GA the first time in 1981. It was the first time I saw

how the rest of the world existed and I NEVER wanted to go back to Buffalo after that. The one thing that I will never forget is the mindset. People who were so set in their ways that nothing could ever change their minds. Not life or death. I had such a disdain for the Towne Gardens that I made a promise to myself to do everything I could never to have to return. Nevertheless, I did learn a lot about my own culture in the Towne Gardens. I learned that when a culture has been marginalized, it can destroy the culture's collective dreams and goals. Thus this is where the terms "crabs in the barrel" is most appropriate. What we can't see for ourselves, we refuse to see for other people.

Some people were obviously never going to leave a one-mile radius of the Towne Gardens and others who had a lot of talent but would eventually succumb to this small mindset and remain there as well. I left Buffalo 34 years ago and never looked back except to visit family which for many years I dreaded doing as well. I wanted no part of that city and 34 years later I STILL have never missed Buffalo or anything about it.

Recently, I went back to visit and saw the house that I grew up in. The memories are still there, and the apartment is now being used as a storage unit, but it is just as I remember it – except it seems smaller. If you want to gain a fresh perspective on how far you have come, visit where you came FROM, and you will be able to see it instantly. My mother never left that area and still lives there today, and she has a lot of love for it that I never had.

When I was a child, I watched my mother get up at 5 AM each day and go to a job she absolutely hated. She was incredibly frustrated and had to go out in single digit freezing temperatures to go to a job and work for a university system that was incredibly racist. She did that for 25 years, and I remember telling myself while hearing her raise her voice in frustration each morning, I NEVER want to be in that position. I NEVER want to work for people who hate me, and I NEVER want to work for people I don't like. It became my life's mission. Initially, I wanted to become a huge star, and I had/have the talent to do it.

Moving to LA

When I moved to Los Angeles in 1990, I worked for a magazine called Urban Network. It was the industry standard for a radio publication or, as we called it, a trade publication, which targeted radio program directors around the country. It was not what I wanted to do at all; I wanted to sing and act. One of the greatest mistakes I have ever made was not going after my dream directly and using side streets to get the main street. I wasted a LOT of time doing that but ultimately, perhaps it was in the cards because I saw how the industry machine really worked and came to realize very quickly that talent was only a minute part of the equation, hell it wasn't even a

Mind Your Own Damn Business

requirement in many cases. I've never been one for politics or kissing the asses of people I despised or had disdain for because of my upbringing. I also hate bullies, and I found the music and radio industry was full of them. When I worked for the Urban Network, there was a ton of dissension. There were people who were there who should not have been there, who did not work there and who the industry was done with and had thrown away –

and it became easy to see why. They were often bitter and brought their toxicity to the organization and Urban Network was no longer a fun place to work but it turned into a battle zone. One that was consumed by infighting most of the time. But for me, everything that you have read before this proved to be incredibly valuable at the end of the day. This was the first lesson I learned about surrounding yourself with the best or the worst team. Negativity is like stage IV cancer, once it's into the bloodstream of the organization, the lifespan is shortened. I also came to realize that negative people are incredibly powerful. Much more so than positive people because it's such a heavy energy.

At the time the industry was changing, as it does every decade, as a new breed of people were coming in. In my mid-20s, I was in that new breed of people. The one thing that I learned very quickly was that my journey would be tough and, at times, seemingly impossible. I never had a mentor or anyone to take me under their wing to show me the ropes. There was a time that I deeply regretted that but, as I got older, I realized it was the best thing that could've happened. And had I had a mentor I may have never stepped out of my own to do what I do today. When I mentor younger people now, I tell them to run their own companies.

When I was working in the Urban Network, and all the infighting was taking place, all of the older industry people were battling each other for power by any means necessary, stabbing each other in the back betraying each other and even getting the younger people involved by picking on us to get information. The whole situation made no sense to me; it was a waste of time and energy. And I knew it was a matter of time before I got fired after getting caught up in the bullshit politics, so I disconnected myself from it and focused on a better future (the same thing I did growing up in the Towne Gardens). Sometimes you just have to let things take place and not invest in it. Eventually anything negative will collapse. You have to ask yourself if you want to collapse with it.

No Experience is a Bad Experience if there is an Education Behind it

Some of the lessons that I learned from the Urban Network have proven precious to me, nevertheless, since I started my own business. For example, after being assigned as a rap editor – a job I absolutely hated – I was also assigned to fulfill a sales role. This was a blessing. On top of that, the boss upstairs demanded that I collect payments (another blessing). At that point, I thought to myself; I'm basically running my own business. And when the checks would come in for anywhere between five and $10,000, I was getting a small 10% cut. 20% was the standard for salespeople, but I was only getting 10%. Part of my problem when I was younger was that I did not see my own value and, if there's something that I tell younger people today more than anything else, that is if you don't see your own value it will be determined for you and it will always be a LOT less than it actually is.

Starting My Business...

Urban Network fired me in 1992 but unbeknownst to them; I GRADUATED in 1992 from Urban Network. I learned everything I needed to get to run my own business and didn't even realize it. I spent all my time learning while they were fighting. I volunteered to do extra work, KNOWING it would not matter to them but would benefit me. I truly did not know I was setting myself up for success, but the universe was setting me up because I was doing the work. I started "Radio Fax" which is what it was then called in 1995, after working at a few radio stations after being fired from Urban Network as a DJ. This one particular programmer really had it in for me, but he was brutal to everyone else too. I was being bullied at the radio station in Los Angeles. At the time I was in my early 30s, the youngest member of staff and I hated playing music from the 50s and 60s. I didn't relate to it, and it was boring and, to be honest, I never wanted to be a DJ. But even that situation opened the doors further for my business. I was a DJ because I could do it and not because I wanted to do it. It was a way to get closer to singing and I always thought,

Mind Your Own Damn Business

when I played someone else's record, that someone should be playing my record. I didn't want to be just the liaison between the artist and the audience; I wanted to be the artist himself. Knowing this, I retired from radio in 1999 in my mid-30s. I figured that I would leave the role for someone who actually wanted to do it. To that end, this was another situation that worked out to my advantage. I stayed in radio under the unions (very few urban stations are union stations or provide retirement for radio DJs) just long enough, I mean literally, a couple of weeks out of a seven year period to get vested. I didn't find this out for many years later, but I was glad to hear it.

If there's one thing I learned in life, it is that things that seem bad are not necessarily bad if they become lessons. Especially if we survive them; the boss I had that was a bully was jealous of me. At the time I didn't know it because I had never experienced such negativity. I have never been jealous of anyone, so I didn't understand anyone being jealous *of me*. But he did really crazy things to hold me back from progressing. Like giving me bad job references for stations that were calling trying to hire me. He would tell me, after they called, that I should've let him know they were going to call and he would've been better prepared. But how was I supposed to know they would call? He was protecting himself and the station from being sued, but at the time, once again, I was very naïve to this kind of thing because I just wanted to get along with everybody and do my job. In the end, his jealousy became so incredibly innate that it pushed me in a direction I never thought I would go.

Not Paying Rent

The old saying is true that once you have hit bottom there

is nowhere to go but up. At this point, I was at the bottom. I stopped my beat up car at a pawn shop in Hollywood one day in 1995 and walked in to find a record player for my vinyl. The first thing I saw was a Mac computer from around 1995. It was truly antiquated, but I was immediately drawn to it. It cost $600.00 which was cheap for a computer in those days, ,so I bought it with my rent money. Almost without a second thought.

I would write about my experiences; the only way to relieve myself my distress. One day I took a chance and faxed out an editorial about the music industry and my thoughts, and I sent it to about 20 people. I could not sleep. I heard the fax machine going all night on the computer, and I was thinking to myself "what am I doing? What's going to happen to my career?" The editorial was full of anger and frustration, and the thought of being blackballed didn't matter anymore. I had to let it out and send it out to the world. The response was phenomenal. I got calls and emails the next day ALL day, and I was repeatedly being told I had to keep it up. People were hungry for someone with a voice for the voiceless. So I did.

In another failed effort to get this boss to like me, I showed him my new newsletter Radio Fax. I was very proud. I could tell he had heard about it, but he never said anything to me. He threw my newsletter across his desk and said: "What are you gonna do with that shit!" At that point, I realized I had not paid attention to a very hard lesson the Towne Gardens had taught me when a person hates themselves, and they are jealous, the nicer you are to them the MORE they hate you, especially when you are trying to make peace. Success is ALWAYS the BEST revenge. It's the one thing they want LEAST for you

Mind Your Own Damn Business

because they see it coming your way, perhaps before you do.

The End of the Bullshit

One day, another station in town had offered me a job, but this time they called me directly. I wanted to talk to this boss about it before the staff meeting, as I wasn't sure what I was going to do. We left it at that. I told him I would let him know. Then we went to the staff meeting, and the first thing he said was Kevin Ross has an announcement to make, everyone immediately looked at me, I was frozen in my tracks. They KNEW I had been set up, but I had very little time to react. Should I go off, attack him, walk out, play it off... WHAT? I made the announcement that I was leaving. I'm SO glad I picked that option. I could have gone off, and I'm sure I could have sued the station and gotten him fired, but that was not where my energy was at that point. I knew inevitable, under his guise the station would collapse, and several months later it did. Still, it was the most underhanded dirty thing anybody had ever done to me in my entire career. Instead of responding, I took my energy and anger and went to my Mac computer that had purchased from the pawnshop with my rent money, and I wrote it out. That was my next newsletter; I roasted him in a way that I'm sure he never expected. I'm also sure it came back to him. The old saying is true; the pen is mightier than the sword. He said something very negative about me to a couple of people at my new job, and I called HIS boss this time and told him if I heard anything else that he says about me, I would sue the shit out of the station. I was walking in a power that I had never realized before. The GM (his boss) begged me to do a conference call with three black men to work it out. I told the GM, someone, that I had great respect for "Fuck him, I don't want to talk to him about shit, but tell him to keep his fucking mouth shut." I had a lot of nerve, I was lambasting him in my newsletter but demanded he be quiet, and now HE takes the beating. I had heard rumors at the time that the station was in trouble and was about to be extinct. It is exactly what happened. A letter was faxed to the industry shortly after that asking people to make donations to this former boss who was having a hard time financially. While others gloated in his demise, I instinctively knew it was not a good idea. I was enjoying success now with a full on magazine with ads from all the major record labels. I had an office with employees, and I was more successful than

I had ever been working in radio. He was the furthest thing from my mind. I didn't contribute any money, but I didn't gloat either.

This is how a business is born; you find a hole – and then fill it and use life's leverage as an asset. After I purchased that Mac computer from the pawn shop, my rent had not been paid for two months. There were no postings on my door to pay or quit, but I knew it was coming. I got a call from Columbia records the very next day. They wanted to buy three ads, I was shocked, I gave them my price (enough to pay my rent), and the rep laughed. He quadrupled my asking price. I had made an investment in myself that now not only paid the rent for the past two months but now for the rest of the year, and I had a new job. My OWN business. I was immediately in love with the concept. Everything fell into order, and it was supposed to happen that way. It was fate. That was 22 years ago.

LESSONS IN BUSINESS

Don't Follow the Leader, BE the Leader...

Whatever business you're in, you've got to take chances. You can't follow people; you must be the leader in what you do to draw business. It is incredibly frightening to step away from the pack, but that's what successful entrepreneurs do. I would strongly suggest that you find groups with people who don't do what you do but who understand business and talk to them about the challenges, ideas, and concepts you have. Do not talk to everyday people who will never understand you. The minute you stop learning and stop growing, you will stop doing. You'll never be in a position where you're bored with your business. That can be disastrous. If you are bored with your business, it's time to grow in another direction or to bring other people in while you do something else. Often this comes from your industry going in another direction, which is something that can happen anytime. But you have to be prepared to make decisions. Don't be afraid to go in another direction or to educate yourself, to go to conferences or to learn and grow. Knowing that I left radio as a DJ for good in 2000. I was just not interested; I reflected that I had spent 17 years doing radio when my real interest is in the music industry. So I recently made a decision to drastically change my business.

Mind Your Own Damn Business

Don't Allow People to Pimp Your Business

Just as I stated early on about value, if you don't see your value then other people determine it for you, and generally it will work in their favor and not yours. Even today, people still try to pimp my business. Just recently, someone called me and told me that someone had asked for my number. He then went on to say that this person asked for a reference about my business and he said he spoke highly of me. What he didn't realize was that the person who actually ordered the person to buy my business had already talked to me. This person makes a call for my information because they didn't want to call the person giving them the business as it would've made them look like didn't know me. But the person who told me that he gave me a good reference was being dishonest. There was no need to give me a reference; the business had already been purchased. I have caught the same person carrying out numerous transactions, where he was taking money out of my pocket after telling his clients that I had charged a 100% rate, then he would come back and give me 30% while claiming the client didn't have any budget. His job was to keep me away from his client to make sure he could make his cut. I have a problem giving someone a cut of 75% and 80% is unheard off.

It's all in the Presentation...

This is probably one of the MOST important things you will see in this guide. P-R-E-S-E-N-T-A-T-I-O-N!
I don't care what kind of business you have if you don't

present it, yourself or your documents right, you are almost certainly DESTINED to fail. The first line of presentation is your idea. Just the other day a gentleman called me with an idea he had for a magazine. He was all over the place. I kept asking him if he had a business plan – you really don't need a FULL plan, something I will talk about later. I also asked him about startup capital. He kept skirting around the questions. I asked him about investors, and he didn't trust anyone. As he went on and on about how he was going to get his business off the ground and the team he had in place, I lost interest. His lack of direction just sounded like someone mumbling after a while. It sounded like he was confused... and, if he sounds that way to me, how will he handle the business and how will he sound to anyone else that he presents this idea to? He made several common mistakes that potential black business owners make; they are as follows:

Kevin Ross

Beware of Hiring Friends

When Emotion is Involved, Poor Decisions are Made.

You are trying to help them but are they trying to help themselves? If your reason for hiring a friend is to help them financially, instead of loaning them money you may never get back, you are making a mistake. You should be helping YOURSELF first THEN helping them; not the other way around (click "Next" above or below to see next segment). Friends Know your Weaknesses, And they will use them against you in business. They won't think it's malicious but you will. Friends Make you Feel Obligated; You put yourself in a weak position when you hire a friend MOSTLY because of this... YOU make you feel Obligated.

Your intentions are good, but you soon realize you've

made a mistake and now you have to pay more either in money or time to fix it. You Hesitate to Express Dismay You; want to make them as comfortable as possible but why? You Sacrifice the Time and Money because You Don't want to lose the Friendship.

You have bitten off more than you can chew but at this point, it's too late. You have to find a way to get out of the mess that you put yourself in. You are more considerate for friends than you are for other employees. If your employees see this, it will certainly cause dissension and strife, which could end up being a much bigger problem for you. Friends Expect you to give them breaks.

They are only concerned about their own situation, and it makes sense; it is paramount to them at this time, and you are secondary. They will make excuses and Expect you to Understand. After all, you knew they were having financial problems so what's YOUR problem? The whole thing was a complete waste of time. Now you may have a better understanding of why they are broke, and in the situation, they were in in the first place. The lines between Friend and Employee and Boss are blurred. Knowing this now and you will realize it was best to simply GIVE them the money. Good luck. There is a sense of entitlement and disrespect disguised as a pat on the back and respect.

Be careful who you surround yourself with in front of your clients

I had a situation a few years back where I took a "friend" to an event because she was out of work and I knew there would be people there that could help her get back into her field. The VP of the company wanted me to ride with him to the event, and I sat in the lobby with her while he got dressed. When the VP came downstairs and was ready to go, she complained that her feet were hurting and we were walking too fast. FIRST WARNING! We get to the event after the VP, and I slow down for her, and she speaks to everybody, and she had a drink which leads to another drink and another drink. She gets drunk, and I can hear her slurring her words and speaking loudly while I'm talking to colleagues on the balcony. SECOND WARNING. I pull her to the side and tell her "You are drunk and you are talking too loud; bring it down a few notches. She agrees, and 10 minutes later she is even louder. THIRD WARNING. I am HUMILIATED and EMBARRASSED, and my client is being cordial, but I can tell he is not impressed. I opt to leave the event early just to get her out of there. As we leave, she goes for the final coup-de-gras and asks several people for their cards. I was MORTIFIED as they all lied and said they didn't bring any cards. FOURTH WARNING. We leave, and she takes off her shoes and is complaining about her feet again as we end up in a coffee shop and she is now fully drunk. I can't believe I invited her and I KNEW she had a drinking problem, but I was trying to help her get a job. The next day at another event, I had one glass of wine to try to relax after the mishap the night before, and I got tipsy myself. I usually don't drink. Now I have made my OWN impression. While the client still does business with me, they have not invited me to any of their events since for three years. I mentioned to her that she made a fool of herself and I was trying to help her, and she did what people like her do; she told me I was over thinking it and that I should not care what the client thinks. I should have never expected an alcoholic to take responsibility, especially when she then stated she was not that drunk.

LESSON LEARNED: I have a bad habit of always looking out for others even to the detriment of myself. I should

Mind Your Own Damn Business

have escorted her back to her car and sent her BACK home when she complained about her feet and wanted the client to wait while she tried to maneuver in high heels that she could not wear. All of this could have been avoided if I had stopped everything right there or not invited her at all, knowing her history – which I did. I have to take full responsibility for this grave error for trying to help a "friend" out. I put a friend in quotes because we have to KNOW who our true friends are as small business owners. Some people ACT like they are your friend to go along for the ride, to reap some of the benefits of your hard work, to pick your brain and drain you. My uncle told me when I was a boy that you must always make sure you deal with people in just about every circumstance, who have as much to lose AS YOU DO. That's how you establish trust. He was right, another entrepreneur who was in the same field as me would have thought twice about doing what this woman did. I had to realize that most people are in the situations they are in by CHOICE. They don't want to make the necessary moves to get out of a rut, and we are not their babysitters. Some of us have been there too. You can't lay your burdens on other people if YOU are not willing to do the work FIRST. Truth be told, this woman is an alcoholic and people who have addictions put the addiction ahead of everything else. Being her friend was too much weight on me, so I had to let her go after a couple of other really negative experiences with her. When it comes to doing business, make sure you surround yourself with people who have YOUR best interests in mind along with theirs and not just theirs.

Take a Vacation

I RARELY do this, but it is SO important. The more you

work, the harder it is to leave your business in the hands of others. You fear that they will destroy your business, but that's rarely the case. Your business can survive for a few days without you, and the benefit is that, when you get back, you are ready to take on your job with a new perspective, fresh eyes, and renewed energy. You can even take a mini vacation in a nice resort, in part of your city for a few days, or somewhere else close.

Three years ago, I had this great idea to do a podcast on a regular basis on my main site Radio Facts (www.radiofacts.com). I started putting the show together and assembled a team that I thought would work. I respected their tenure, they were intelligent, and they had various personalities. Most were in between gigs, and I thought it was a great way to put them in front of industry opportunities. I told them to give me 10 weeks of shows before I could start marketing with my own contacts to try to sell it. They all agreed at the onset. Two weeks into the show, some members of the team started asking me for money. They were doing this in front of other members. While I believed in the idea, there were other factors that made me think twice before putting my own money up. They wanted to be paid for their time, but they were not hungry, and they didn't see my vision. They wanted me to take some of the money from my main business to pay them for their time. I had to ask myself if I was being fair. While I respected their time, my main business had nothing to do with the new one and, if the Podcasts made money, I would have taken the money back that I gave them [invested] and they would not have appreciated that. So I didn't think it was a good idea. Also, they were not using their forums (social media) to promote the podcasts that we had done, so I was doing the recording, paying for and setting up the conference calls, editing (which was a HUGE job) the show and the marketing as well. They were only involved in the calls. There was not enough hunger or passion and, while I understand people have to pay bills, I concluded that this idea was not going to be in the best interest for any of us and I didn't want to end up coming off as the bad guy. I saw the negativity starting to build, and it was time to back out.

If I Got a Penny for Every Great Idea, I Gave Away for Nothing...

To cut a long story short, some of the members continued to point out that I was getting quite a bit of advertising on my main site. I felt my money for a business that I had built from the ground up — on my own — was being scrutinized and counted. I was not comfortable with that, but I got their point too. I ended up canceling the group concept of the show and did a couple of segments on my own with my remaining energy. Ironically, the ones that I did on my own received more downloads. One vignette that was brief – consisting of me giving simple advice – got over 600,000 downloads (www.radiofacts.podbean.com). None of the group podcasts had even come close to that. I had to retool the idea and, while I will have other hosts, I lost three years of lead time for a successful podcast site waiting for others to come on board and see my vision. It was a case of trying to lead the horse to water that refused to drink. I lost my energy to carry on when it became a "job" instead of a passion, as I'm sure other entrepreneurs understand.

In another instance, I was also the member of a mindshare group that I didn't start but was invited to join. The group had the potential to reach a greater amount of entrepreneurs, using events to earn income, as we all had incredible potential to teach others. I proposed the idea several times, and it was constantly poo-pooed by the other members who claimed they had other things to do with their time, yet they were all constantly trying to find ways to increase their income.

After a couple of months, we started getting announcements of events hosted by people with MUCH less experience, who had sponsors and were doing exactly what I had proposed. The group then pointed out "Perhaps we should do something like this!" I was shocked but maintained my composure. However, I immediately lost interest in being involved at that point. You grow tired of being the gift horse. Some of us have excellent ideas that never go anywhere when we depend on others to implement, assist and give birth to them. It can take more energy to organize people to see your vision than it would to simply do it on your own. There are better ways to utilize your ideas and time.

You Kill the Energy When you Give it Away

Keep in mind, WHEN your idea is not well received by others, or it is questioned or scrutinized, the balloon loses its air current, meaning your concept is without a lift. When you back down and shut up, you should also consider moving on. As with any relationship when your ideas are constantly shut down, you SHOULD question the relationship and whether or not it's right for you. The answer is almost always NO.

People Don't (Won't, Can't) See what you See

I have found, when it comes to black folks especially, that we respond to crisis best. We are a very emotional community when it comes to things like racism, but we are very relaxed as a community when it comes to things like entrepreneurs, investing (in ourselves) and long-term strategies. You can't make someone walk when they would rather drive a broken down dangerous vehicle that's a fire hazard. If they want to drive they will drive, UNTIL the vehicle catches fire while they are driving it.

Stop Taking People Where They Don't Want to Go

Ask or suggest just the once. If you KNOW that you are the idea guy or girl and you are ignored, go where you will be appreciated but stop swimming in shallow waters.

You Will Frustrate Yourself

Having a great idea shows your savviness and ability to grow. When someone shoots it down or attacks, or questions the concept, there is no need to continue to try to get them to see what they will never see. THEY will win, and you will become complacent and a follower like them. If you are a leader, you have to also LEAD yourself into better, more productive environments that HELP you grow, not SHRINK or remain stagnant.

It's Not Your Job to Save the World

While the idea guy may have some brilliant ideas, some people are comfortable suffering. Leave them where they are, and perhaps they will see you on the way up and join in, that's the best that you can hope for but don't let their negative concepts stop YOU.

If People Ask For Your Help then Don't Use Your Ideas, MOVE ON

Nuff said. Stop wasting your time.

Mind Your Own Damn Business

One of the greatest complaints and challenges in business is almost always money. We rarely consider the REAL reasons we don't make money, but it goes BEYOND "the Economy" or "Budgets." Truth be told, clients will always FIND money for services they believe in. Also, consider that there are small businesses who do absolutely NO selling and make all the money they need and more BECAUSE they are doing one or all of the things below (click Next above or below to see the next segment).

Look at what you are producing. Are you up to date?

This is a HUGE mistake I have seen people make in the music industry and in my business. The music industry is very fast paced, and things can literally change from week-to-week. Many small businesses in the industry are not up to date. They are run by one person who doesn't have the staff and who constantly uses excuses about not hiring anyone because they don't have the extra money. Most of the time we DO have the money, even for assignment based jobs, but we are often cheap and greedy, and we don't want to share our profits. There are some people who legitimately need the money, but most people I come across could cut out the Cable they never watch at home and put that money into building their brands. You will NEVER have the extra money if you are not up to date and if you don't SPEND some to make some (wisely of course). Hiring family is not a good idea because they may or may not want to do what YOU do and it creates problems. Hire someone even part-time or on assignment who is strong where you are weak. If you are not able to keep up with current trends in your industry, it will be very obvious in what you produce. Don't take that chance because, once you are labeled "dated," you are just that and potential clients will lose interest in you.

Stop using your Tenure

People who use their tenure to bully clients into buying are mere crybabies. Your tenure is meaningless if you are dated and at times it can work AGAINST you because you will appear OLD. I have had this problem for years with competitors who ALWAYS call my clients whenever they see an ad on my site or in my publications. They moan and groan like kids in a playground about being left out and how they have worked so many years in the industry and should have the same benefit as my brands do but they never do the work. They copy and steal from others (including me) and want their own credit for it. They do that because their products suck and the clients often come back and tell me this. Focus on the product FIRST. What is it that you can do that nobody else, even competitors, can't do? If you can't come up with anything, like my competitors can't, you will rely on whining and belly aching about being left out like it's a child's baseball game and you were the last to be chosen. Clients are outrageously annoyed by business owners like this and, if you have to struggle, especially after your first year in business and you don't have several regular clients... something is wrong.

Use Social Media Networks

I am a HUGE social media person with my business, and it works to my advantage because most, if not all, of my competitors have never taken the time to learn or understand how important social media is. We are all over 40, but that doesn't mean we can't be on top of the trends, though some people are lazy. I will tell you, if you want to earn more you have to be more and DO more and part of that is constantly branding your product. Social media doesn't have to be a chore and it can actually be automated by using a few services while you work. There are also apps for retailers that can either film you working or help keep customers up to date to check out your services.

Stop comparing yourself to others

I had a boss that once told me that, if you are in a race and you look to either side of you, you lose time... He said to only focus on the finish line. I have to agree. When you look at what someone else is doing AND you compare yourself to them, it speaks volumes for your services or what you lack. What can you do BETTER or how can you provide more appealing services to your clients? Stop copying and come up with your OWN way of promoting and succeeding with your brand.

Upsell Your Current Clients

Chasing dead clients is a waste of time. There are some clients who will NEVER support you. Stop calling them and asking them to support you and focus on your current clients, who will probably be willing to spend even MORE money with you if you have something ELSE to offer of value. Don't try to raise your rates on them; you may lose them if you do that.

Mind Your Own Damn Business

How Can you Improve?

Having a business is not only about working, but it's also about researching new trends and educating yourself. Are you doing that? Some entrepreneurs work WAY too many hours a day, especially those with mobile businesses. Check out Groupon and Meet-ups for meetings that will help you network with other entrepreneurs so that you can learn more about what's going on in your industry.

Send out an email blast

Do you have a new product? What's the latest news with your business? I can't tell you how many new clients I have gotten via email blasts that I do daily. People pass your email blasts around, and it's a great way to keep your brand in the minds of others and to make more revenue. Give your email blasts some added value talk about something of interest to your client base and industry. Give them some tips or news; they LOVE it.

Attend Conferences where your Clients go

There are literally hundreds of conferences every year. I go to a few vital ones to meet potential clients face to face. I like to meet marketing people at various corporations. I don't like gatekeepers and middlemen, they ALWAYS get in the way of your success, so find a way to get around THEM. People will do business with you because they like you and believe in you. They can't do that if they don't

KNOW you.

Get a feature in a POPULAR Blog in your field

Write press releases about your business or new products. There are services like PRWeb that will put your press release in front of thousands of bloggers, websites, magazines and newspapers. Are you using them?

Get Testimonials from Satisfied Customers

This is an excellentway to garner MORE interest in your product. Use this at all times and make sure you rotate, especially interest from well-known people.

Being an entrepreneur is incredibly rewarding. Unfortunately, there are other aspects of it that are very challenging. When you're the boss, it is often difficult to have leverage or camaraderie with people that work for you. You have to maintain a level of authority. Most of the time, entrepreneurs, surround themselves with other entrepreneurs because they understand each other best.

Working for yourself is and is not what people think. You do not sit around idly twiddling your thumbs waiting for money to pour in all day long with no effort... it's work and nonstop work. While other people punch the clock at 5 o'clock, entrepreneurs continue to work throughout the day and night.

At times, some of the best ideas come to entrepreneurs in

Mind Your Own Damn Business

the middle of the night. We don't always feel like motivating ourselves at this period, but it is essential to our success. After 21 years, here are some tips I can share with you on lessons that I have learned the hard way. You're welcome... (LOL). Click NEXT above or below for next segment.

Create Win/Win/WIN Situations...

First and foremost, you have to be absolutely sure that you have a winning product. It's hard to believe in or convince others to believe in crap. They can plainly see the value of what you do. Your customers are interested in your product. Always think of the three "WINS": 1. How is this going to benefit my business? 2. How is this going to benefit the client?, and 3. How is it going to benefit the target? The "target" can be anything from a specific target to potential new clients who see what you produce. Therefore, WHAT you produce must be stellar so that others are attracted to it. If you're just taking money, living off tenure or you're not delivering services, you probably won't see the client again no matter what kind of business you are in. Repeat business, without suggestion or solicitation, is the key. There has to be balanced in order to create and sustain a valuable and longstanding relationship. Don't be greedy and think you can get the money this time, deliver a crappy service then expect the client to return. Not only will they not return, but they will also tell others how they were treated.

Stop Hiring People Who NEED a

Mind Your Own Damn Business Job!

What do I mean by that? I'm basically saying that sometimes, as entrepreneurs, we ask our contacts if they know someone who can do so and so and we really need the job done but don't have the time to look for potential candidates. Don't make this mistake. I have found that in at least 80% of the time in situations like these, the people don't work out. Mostly, because they don't "WANT" a job, they NEED a job. Therefore they are only going to give you enough effort to make money then they are gone. Unfortunately, when they don't work out, and you have wasted your time training them, YOU become the bad guy if you complain and it could affect your relationship with the original person you asked for help from. Chances are if they are trying to help a friend or relative that needs a job, this does not work for you or your business. You're not a temp service looking for day laborers. You have to look at your business, and what it needs, that's the primary consideration. You need someone that WANTS a job, not someone who is going to do just enough to get by and then hit the road. Anything less just won't do. Wasting time is not a good idea for your business. You want to make sure that you bring in someone who's hungry and wants the job. Some people say that there are no hungry people anymore, but there are. You just have to dig deeper and find them and, even if they're not hungry, at least make sure they're strategic, and they know what they're doing, and they're effective because you can still get the same benefits. Don't always be obligated to hire people because they need a job; hire them for WHY you NEED them.

Don't be afraid to ask for what you want...

When it comes to your business, you have to take care of it and protect it. Do not be afraid to approach people for what you want when it comes to your business. If you need help – and this is the most important thing – don't be afraid to ask. If you don't know something, don't be afraid to admit but make sure you learn at least a little bit of it so that you can keep an eye on all aspects of your business. When hiring someone to do an independent job, check their credentials and have them send you some of that work and then take the time to dig a little deeper. Look at their social networks to get an idea of their character. I would not recommend hiring a third-party with someone in the middle who is speaking for the other person. This indicates that the person you're talking to is taking the largest chunk of the money and only giving a small portion to the third-party. That's a waste of your resources. Hire direct. If you never have contact with the third-party you can't know how effective they are. I've made this mistake a few times too many, but not anymore.

Why is it so hard to find good people?

That's a very good question? And there is some truth to it. But we must first realize that nobody is going to have the passion and the drive that we have for our business to succeed. I would strongly suggest that you have a layout for whatever project you have, showing the person exactly what you expect them to do and have them sign it. It could be the 10 steps you want them to take, or it could be just a general synopsis of what you expect. Otherwise, they don't have a guide, and you may be disappointed with the final results. On occasion, you will come across someone who does a great job and who is dedicated to doing exactly what you want them to do. Make sure that you keep these people in your database to call when you need certain things. There is a good chance that they can do even more tasks than you asked them for the first time. You must establish a solid team, and sometimes it takes a lot of trial and error to get there.

Enjoy the fruits of your labor

As entrepreneurs, especially black entrepreneurs, we have

a tendency to work ourselves to death early on or until we die. Radio One owner Cathy Hughes pointed out to me during a recent interview that when we leave our businesses to our children, by the time we leave it, they usually don't want it. We have literally worked ourselves to death and not traveled the world or taken the time off that we should have taken just to have the business die with us. I cannot tell you how many times I have seen black owners work themselves to death by not taking care of themselves in the process. I must admit, running a business is addictive, and at times it's very difficult to walk away, but you MUST find a way to enjoy the fruits of your labor. Don't be in a position where you are not taking vacations, not having sustained relationships, with only work, work, work. You're an entrepreneur because you want the freedom to do what you want to do. It would seem that would include taking a vacation and having free time to do the things that you love to do, but others can't do because they're obligated to go to work each day. I know someone who works on a blog and puts in 16 hour days. He's older than me; he never leaves home except to go to an event here and there that is related to his blog and he is very unhappy. He has not had a vacation in years; he's not making a lot of money because he doesn't focus on sales and his target is oversaturated, so he has to work harder to keep up. I understand the fear that you think that, if you leave, something will happen and you won't be on top of it, but that's the beauty of technology. Especially with a blog, you can actually post from anywhere in the world with your iPhone. Life is too short not to enjoy being an entrepreneur and reaping the benefits.

Kevin Ross

Take care of yourself, have a "ME" day.

The beauty of management is that you have the free time to do things that other people can't do at the same time. Going to the grocery store during the day is wonderful because there are no lines. Driving around with no traffic is great. Going to a restaurant when it's empty with a friend or a client. Take at least one day out of the week to enjoy the fruits of your labor again; go catch the latest movie or matinée when it's cheaper and empty; go to the restaurant you want to go to; take a trip to the museum to see the exhibits you want to see; go and lay out on the beach, though you have to leave your phone and enjoy yourself after a while as this will become a habit. I know someone who is desperately looking for love, but he's always working. The irony of it is that everything that he wants in a relationship comes his way but, while he's working, he's so motivated to make money that he pushes it away and then wonders why it's not around when he slows down. The universe is attracted to what's moving, not what is standing still. If life were a race, people would cheer on the person running for the finish line. They don't cheer on the people on the sidelines. Decide what your position is and "run" with it.

Grow your business...

Things will not always be as they are right now. People change jobs and clients change their minds and companies downsize or eliminate budgets. Why should you settle for having two or three clients when you can have 30 for more sustainability? That doesn't mean that you have to continue to do what you're doing, especially when there's limited growth potential. You must create an additional ancillary product to grow your business and brand. Can you do an event? A conference, a magazine, a blog for your clients or customers? You have to decide but don't stand still while the going is good because it won't always be that way, trust me, and you want to have as many repeat clients as possible. Do your best to create multiple streams of income. Even if it's from your original idea that you can grow or multiple ideas that can work themselves. The ideal income is the one that comes in while you sleep. There is no greater feeling than getting up in the morning and seeing that people around the world have paid for your services and you were not even there.

Mind Your Own Damn Business

Eliminate People who Drain your Mental Resources

You can't be friends with everyone; you don't owe anyone anything and, when people make you feel like shit, flush them down the toilet. It's that simple, and it's a great mental concept. You know who they are because you feel drained when you finish talking to them and they demand too much of your dedication, attention, and energy. Keep your life as simple as possible and surround yourself with like-minded easy going people. Find other activities to cope with boredom instead of picking up the phone and calling people who drain you. This is not only "friends"; it could also be family. Everyone is not going to be happy for you when you are successful.

Tale of Two Legendary Restaurants; One that still is and

Kevin Ross

ONE that WAS.

I left Buffalo, New York some 30 years ago and, once I moved to Atlanta then Los Angeles after that and worked in radio as a DJ for many years, there was no turning back. The new environments opened my eyes to all that I had missed growing up on the East Side of Buffalo. Nevertheless, there is one thing that is foremost in my mind on the few occasions when I return, think or talk about Buffalo... the food. Without question, my career in the music industry has afforded me the opportunity to go to some of the best restaurants in the country, but none of them compare to Buffalo's still famous food spots.

Scottie's Steak House popped on the scene in the early 60s in Buffalo (see video). Owner James Scott explains everything that we know it takes as entrepreneurs to run a successful business and get it off the ground. As a radio and music industry entrepreneur, I can agree even today with MOST of Scott's points in the video but not all of them. He makes two statements that probably explain why his restaurant is no longer around today. He states that "Owning your own business is not fun." Says who? The old adage is true, "Do what you LOVE, and the money will COME." An entrepreneur going into a business he or she is not passionate about is almost sure to fail. Running your own business that you are passionate about is like falling in love. Time slips away, and you can spend endless hours doing what you do and not even notice you have been doing it for 10 hours straight. That is the bliss of doing what you love. Scott mentions on the video that he has worked 18 hour days. I know music producers who LIVE in the studio and can do it for several days straight, with little or no sleep. I never hear them complain about how many hours they have been in the studio; they are more focused on the result of it. The number one rule is you NEVER go into business to make money (unless you have an excellent business partner who handles that part and you are the creative ebb and flow). Most of the people who I know and am close to today are entrepreneurs, and they are all successful in their own right because they LOVE what they do FIRST and FOREMOST. Our creativity is at its peak when we love what we do, and THAT's what sells our business first.

In the years to come, Scottie's Steak House experienced great success, and it's amazing how the video coverage talks about the local government in Buffalo giving small business loans to blacks back then. They were smart enough to capitalize on the culture and what they knew best, but how much did they love it? This is not a dig on Scottie because I have no doubt he faced many other obstacles that got in the way of him running his business as a black man. Restaurants in the black community were something that white business owners often failed at because they were not connected to the culture of black food. Like most cultures, black folks KNOW when the right cook is in the kitchen, and you better be connected to the culture the food is from if you want our business. (Thanks to Doug Ruffin who told me he stopped Canisius College from dumping many years of great Buffalo News footage and video in the trash after it was donated by local TV networks who were updating their studios. These videos are priceless.)

I'm not sure how Scottie got to his idea for the perfect steak sandwich, but he did. This was the MOST Crucial time for his Business.

Scottie's Steak House had the most amazing steak sandwiches. By far the best I've ever had to date. A childhood friend, Cricket, asked me to walk there with her one day and I wanted to go to see what the big deal was about Scottie's. Everybody in the neighborhood was talking about their steak sandwiches and how good they were. Sure enough, as soon as we walked in the door, it was crowded, and the smell was unbelievable. Cricket ordered a regular steak sandwich/sub, and she gave me a piece of it. It was love at first bite. I went back on my own a few days later, then again the next week and many times after that; I was hooked. Then something happened. I noticed (read more, click here) that the more popular Scottie's Steak House became, the more the sandwiches were changing. There were more vegetables than meat. I watched the girl make my sandwich one day, and I noticed she was putting half the meat on, with more peppers and onions than I was used to. I thought this might just be a new employee and, after a not so enjoyable experience with a "vegetable sandwich," I went back a month later, and there was even LESS meat, and the PRICE went up!!!! It appeared they were using what they once used for one steak sandwich to now make three sandwiches. Where the meat was once the main ingredient, it was now pretty much used for seasoning the sandwich like Lawry's. I never went back, and I noticed there was no crowd the last few times I was there, and people stopped talking about Scottie's like they used to.

On the other hand... Bocce's Pizza

Bocce's website states:

Bocce's Pizza is one of the oldest and best-known pizzerias in Buffalo, NY. Since 1946, we've been proudly serving our customers some of the best-tasting food in Western New York. Our fresh pizza is still made with the same sauce recipe used back in the 1940s.

Our delicious food has touched so many lives throughout the years that we are sought out by many who had to leave the Buffalo area. We get phone calls and have customers come in all the time requesting a half-baked pizza or wings to take home to share with their new friends and family across the country.

Stop by or call today for an Original Bocce's Pizza and let us create a delicious memory for you!

I am here to tell you this statement is the absolute truth. Bocce's original owner was the son of Italian immigrants (cultural connection), and he saw many people come and go, some of whom even started their own pizzerias, but they were loyal enough not to try to duplicate what the original owners did. Bocce's did not have a great location,

Mind Your Own Damn Business

as a matter of fact, it was dilapidated and appeared abandoned (see image), but the pizza was all she wrote about. That damn building could have collapsed while you were ordering your food.

You work hard for what you have, and you have done a great job at holding it together. Don't waste your valuable business time and energy on people who want you to bend over backward to offer them services for free or at outrageous discounts. People of ALL business types will try to pull a fast one on you by asking for unreasonable things that don't help you grow; they actually HURT your business. Keep in mind, IF THEY CONTACT YOU... YOU are in the driver's seat, baby. NOT THEM. Don't give them control of the road that leads to YOU and what you have to offer. Read on... (click "next" after each segment above or below).

Avoid Doing "Favors" in Business

1. What's the Return for lack of investment?

Isn't that an interesting statement? It is because the answer to it is absolutely NOTHING for YOU. If you want to work for free then tell your landlord or mortgage company you want to live for free too... and see what they say.

2. How will this person EVER see the VALUE of something that is Free?

A woman told me this at a business conference, and she was right. You don't have to prove yourself to anyone if you have a legitimate and needed service. Offering your services for free is a HUGE mistake that YOU will never stop paying for.

3. Never Allow a Client to "Test" your Services

People tried this with me early on but, as my business grew, they stopped trying this. If I'm running banners with Alicia Keys and Beyonce on my site, there is no need for me to prove my value to an independent client who has a lesser known client. The ads speak for themselves. If someone comes at me with this BS, the conversation is very short.

4. Don't Give the same price Competitors give if your Service is Better

This really irritates me because potential clients assume you are desperate when they pull this one. First and foremost, I quickly correct them by telling them they get much more value with my brand, THEN I give them numbers to back it up which usually shuts them up (or down). If your service is superior to your competitors' and you can prove it, always have the information handy. Also, take into account if they utilized your competitors' services first THEN they come to you. It's usually because the competitors' services did not deliver and they expect you to cut them a deal when they should have come to you in the first place. Them wasting their money is NOT your responsibility and saving money many times can cost you TWICE as much when you try to cut corners in the advertising game. Perhaps it's the same with your business.

5. What if the "Client" tells others about the break you gave them?

Mind Your Own Damn Business

Chances are THEY WILL. Then you will have prices all over the place. My clients constantly tell me what competitors charge so what would stop them from telling them what I charge?

6. Don't let anyone put your business down (unless it sucks)

This is something that I absolutely won't stand for. I know my value, and it's not based on tenure or ego, it's based on who I reach. I CONSTANTLY do research and try new ways to improve what I do. When a potential client calls for a discount by putting my business down, it's like bad credit. I probably won't take their calls again. Early on, such as approach might work because you may not be too sure about your business and you may lack confidence, but once you DO know your value and you develop the confidence, don't let others shake it. There are some clients you just have to say 'No' to.

Barter ONLY when the benefit is GREATER to you

Barters should always, and I mean ALWAYS, be win/bigger win situations FOR YOUR BENEFIT if the person contacts you. Believe it or not, SEVERAL major corporations have contacted me to do barters as early as last week. Let me get this right... you make millions, and you want to offer me next to (or) nothing to promote your brand? I don't think so. I've had companies literally ask me for $10,000 worth of advertising for a $250.00 admission ticket where I had to pay for my plane fare and hotel. Really? I don't think so. Many sales people at corporations are told to see what they can get free first, and I don't fall for that anymore and neither should you IF you have value (see next statement "What is Value?"). If a client comes at you with a deal where it benefits YOU more than them, then you may want to consider. In my example, if a client needs me to promote their event weeks in advance, they need ME more than I need them and I would rather they pay for the advertising, and I will buy my own admission ticket since I am paying for my plane fare and hotel too. The problem is, I usually don't want to go under these conditions and see no value in it for my audience, so it's not a win/bigger win situation.

Reasons You Should NOT do Favors in Business

PLEASE understand what "Value" in small business is before you assume you have it. "VALUE" is NOT tenure, it is NOT who you know, and it is NOT a hook-up service. While you may be able to use any or all of them at times to make money, TRUE "VALUE" is how well your business does to reach the target, sell to the target or convince the target and the WAY you do it: your consistency, your delivery, your relationships and client satisfaction. If a client does not come back to you with more business after the first time, something is wrong. You should not be in business for YEARS still trying to create new clients and struggling. You should have regular clients. Like a barber, like a grocery store, like cleaners and so on. Value is NOT attacking potential clients for not utilizing your services. Nobody in this business owes you a damn thing. You owe your business the advantage of providing a great service

Mind Your Own Damn Business

to your target and THAT my friends is what "Value" is.

I sincerely hope these tips help you grow your business.

www.ingramcontent.com/pod-product-compliance
Lightning Source LLC
Chambersburg PA
CBHW020929180526
45163CB00007B/2944